This is a Carlton book

Published in 2020 by Carlton Books Limited,
an imprint of the Carlton Publishing Group,
20 Mortimer Street, London W1T 3JW

A catalogue record for this book is available from the British Library.

ISBN: 978-1-78312-503-6

Printed in Dongguan, China

10 9 8 7 6 5 4 3 2 1

Executive Editor: Bryony Davies
Design Manager: Emily Clarke
Designer: WildPixel
Production: Nicola Davey

www.carltonbooks.co.uk

STRANGER PLACES

WRITTEN BY HANNAH WILSON

CARLTON KIDS

CONTENTS

SPOOKY SPOTS AROUND THE WORLD

THE PLACES IN THIS BOOK AREN'T JUST STRANGE, THEY'RE STRANGER THAN ANYWHERE YOU'VE EVER HEARD OF. WE'RE TALKING NATURE'S NASTIES — GLACIERS THAT BLEED, MOUNTAINS THAT EAT PEOPLE, ISLANDS INFESTED WITH DEADLY SNAKES AND BEACHES SUFFOCATED BY GIANT SPIDERWEBS. WE'LL TIPTOE THROUGH TERRIFYING TOWNS AND DECAYING BUILDINGS, PLAGUED BY GHOULISH GHOSTS AND SKELETONS, DARK SECRETS, CREEPY STATUES AND EVEN CREEPIER DOLLS. READY TO GO? ME NEITHER...

TAYLOR GLACIER, ANTARCTICA

BLACK MOUNTAIN, AUSTRALIA

Snake Island, Brazil

JEEPERS CREEPERS
KINDA CREEPY
CRAZY CREEPY
CREEP-O-METER

6

Check out the **CREEP-O-METER** on every page! How spooked are you?

FACT OR FICTION?

Put it this way, there is no proof that ghosts exist, or that aliens have visited Earth, or that 'supernatural' events are taking place. But that doesn't mean there aren't mysteries. And until science can explain these mysteries, it's fun to let imaginations run wild. Throughout history, people have told, and believed, weird and wild spooky stories. But fear not — they're fiction, not fact.

Aitoliko lagoon Beach, Greece

TERRIFYING TERRAIN

PERHAPS YOU LIKE HIKING? MAYBE YOU'RE A NATURE LOVER OR A HAPPY CAMPER? WELL, STRIKE THESE WEIRD WILDERNESSES OFF YOUR HOLIDAY LIST. THEY'RE DANGEROUS, MYSTERIOUS, POSSIBLY HAUNTED AND, WELL... YOU GET THE PICTURE.

TURKMENISTAN

KARAKUM DESERT, TURKMENISTAN

In 1971, geologists searching for oil drilled into the stony ground of Turkmenistan's Karakum Desert. A huge crater, 70 metres wide, cracked open and released so much methane gas that animals nearby suffocated. The scientists set fire to the crater, hoping to burn away the gas quickly. But fifty years later, the 'Door to Hell' is still a raging inferno.

KINDA CREEPY JEEPERS CREEPERS CRAZY CREEPY

5

CREEP-O-METER

FORESTS OF FEAR

IF YOU GO DOWN TO THESE WOODS TODAY YOU'RE SURE TO GET A BIG SURPRISE. A BIG, CREEPY, CROOKED, TWISTY, TANGLED SURPRISE. FOR THESE WEIRD TREES ARE GOING TO GIVE YOU THE HEEBIE-JEEBIES!

POLAND

THE CROOKED FOREST

Deep inside a quiet woodland in northwest Poland, nature has taken a rather peculiar course. Just above the forest floor, the trunks of a hundred pine trees bend in a sharp right-angle and grow horizontally for 1 to 3 metres, before curving upwards again. Did a snowstorm bend the trees? Did someone deliberately shape them to produce curved wood, perhaps for boat-building? No one knows for sure...

INDIA

LIVING BRIDGES

In the misty, mossy jungles of the state of Meghalaya in northern India, tree roots creep and crawl, crossing rivers to form bridges. It is the local villagers who grow these walkways, pulling, twisting and tying the long, bendy roots of rubber trees. Sometimes bamboo scaffolding is built first and the roots trained to spread over it. The bridges grow stronger all the time as the roots sprawl and thicken, knitting their tangled webs into a creepy wonder. Some are 500 years old; others hang 25 metres above the ground.

KINDA CREEPY JEEPERS CREEPERS CRAZY CREEPY

3

CREEP-O-METER

DEADMEN VALLEY

A FEARSOME MOUNTAIN TRIBE ONCE RULED THE REMOTE NAHANNI RIVER VALLEY IN NORTHWEST CANADA. THEN, QUITE SUDDENLY, THE NAHA DISAPPEARED WITHOUT A TRACE, AND SOME SAY THEIR WARRIOR GHOSTS HAUNT THE FORESTS AND MOUNTAINS. OTHERS WHISPER TALES OF EVIL CURSES, ALIEN LIGHTS AND ROAMING BIGFOOT CREATURES. AND LET'S NOT FORGET THE STRANGE STORIES OF THOSE WHO CAME IN SEARCH OF GOLD AND LOST THEIR HEADS. LITERALLY.

HEADLESS GOLD-HUNTERS

In 1905, two brothers, Willie and Frank McLeod, headed into the valley in search of gold. They never returned. When their bodies were found by a river, there was a grisly surprise — their heads were missing. The area was named Deadmen Valley, but that didn't put off Martin Jorgenson, a gold-miner who set up home there in 1917. One terrible day, his cabin mysteriously burnt to the ground. His skeleton was found among the ashes — but his skull was nowhere to be seen.

CANADA

WILLIE MCLEOD

FRANK MCLEOD

DIARY OF A TREASURE HUNTER:

Legend has it that Willie and Frank found a gold mine before they died, and I've come to find it. Twenty people have already died trying. I'm camped where the McLeods' headless bodies were discovered by their brother Charlie in 1908, among the spruce trees by the South Nahanni River. Some say they were found in sleeping bags, others swear the skeletons were tied to trees. This place sure gives me the creeps. I'm leaving tomorrow. I don't have any gold, but at least I've got my head.

EERIE EYES

DO YOU LOVE STRANGE SUPERNATURAL STORIES? WELL, CHECK OUT THESE GIANT 'EYES' THAT PEER OUT FROM THE HOT DUSTY SAHARA DESERT OF NORTH AFRICA, AND THE SOGGY MARSHLANDS OF SOUTH AMERICA. SCIENCE CAN'T SOLVE ALL THEIR MYSTERIES (YET), SO FEEL FREE TO DREAM OF LOST CIVILIZATIONS AND ALIEN BASES!

EYE OF THE SAHARA

At first, it was thought that Mauritania's 40-kilometre-wide 'Richat Structure' was a crater, gouged by an asteroid smashing into the Earth. Now, scientists think a huge dome of layered, volcanic rock, like a giant onion, was pushed up from below. Over millions of years, the dome eroded (wore away) until only the onion rings remained. But the regularity of the circles convinces some that they are the ruins of the fabled lost city of Atlantis!

MAURITANIA

ARGENTINA

THE SPINNING EYE

Floating in the marshes northwest of Argentina's capital, Buenos Aires, is a near-perfect circle of green, 118 metres wide. And that's not all. The island is slowly spinning, some say, inside a circular pool of water that is strangely clear and cold. Until scientists can study it properly, 'The Eye' remains a mystery that inspires alien-hunters. They ponder the possibility that it is an entrance to an alien base, a doorway for UFOs to fly through!

BLACK MOUNTAIN

MYSTERIOUS DISAPPEARANCES? TICK. HOWLING GHOSTS? TICK. DEADLY CREATURES? TICK. DARK, SCARY PLACES? ABSOLUTELY! THIS PILE OF GIANT BLACK BOULDERS, RISING FROM THE FORESTS OF QUEENSLAND, AUSTRALIA, HAS IT ALL.

DEEP DARK UNDERWORLD

About 150 years ago, people started to go missing on Black Mountain — ranchers, gold hunters, police officers, and Sugarfoot Jack, a criminal needing a hideout. It is said the mountain consumed them all, along with their horses and even an entire herd of cattle. Were they bitten by a death adder or crushed by a seven-metre scrub python? Did they fall into a crevice and, if they survived that, get lost in the deep dark labyrinth of passages below the rocks? In the 1880s, searching for a missing rancher, two trackers entered a cave. Only one returned, too spooked to describe the terrible things he had seen...

A GEOLOGIST REPORTS:

With no soil filling the gaps between the rocks, there are deep chasms everywhere. The rocks, some as big as houses, are covered with blue-green algae that paints the grey granite black. The dark colour absorbs heat, and when cool rain falls, the rock cracks — sometimes explosively! That's why the rocks groan and moan at night. Even I'll admit, this noise, along with the wailing wind, does sound a little like the howling of missing souls trapped beneath the mountain...

KINDA CREEPY JEEPERS CREEPERS CRAZY CREEPY

6

CREEP-O-METER

CREEPY CAVES

COMPUTER TRICKERY HAS ADDED TINY PEOPLE TO THIS CRYSTAL PHOTO, RIGHT? WRONG! THE CRYSTALS IN THIS MEXICAN CAVE REALLY ARE THAT BIG! MAMMOTH CAVE, IN KENTUCKY, USA, ALSO HAS MONSTROUS PROPORTIONS — 650 KILOMETRES OF EXPLORED TUNNELS AND CAVERNS BURYING AS DEEP AS A FIVE-STOREY BUILDING. DON'T GET LOST IN THESE DEEP DARK PLACES — THEY'RE FULL OF DANGER AND, SOME SAY, GHOSTS...

THE CAVE OF GIANT CRYSTALS

Near the town of Naica, Mexico, 300 metres underground, a cave is speared with giant crystals up to 11 metres long and 4 metres wide. Discovered by miners in 2000, the selenite crystals formed over at least 500,000 years as a cocktail of water, oxygen and minerals heated and cooled. But this strange cavern, lying above a magma chamber, is brutally hot — almost 50°C. Without protective equipment, humans wouldn't survive more than a few minutes...

MEXICO

USA

MONSTROUS MAMMOTH CAVE

Ghost stories seep from the depths of the world's longest known cave system. Could the cave's deathly history explain why? About 4,000 years ago, Native Americans buried their dead here, and over the years, several explorers have lost their lives. In 1842, a doctor housed 16 tuberculosis patients in the cave, hoping the air would clear their lungs. It didn't work — five died, their bodies laid out on a long flat stone now called Corpse Rock. Some say, the tormented souls of the dead haunt Mammoth Cave.

KINDA CREEPY
JEEPERS CREEPERS
CRAZY CREEPY

3

CREEP-O-METER

SPINE-TINGLING TOWNS

YOU WON'T COMPLAIN ABOUT YOUR BORING OLD HOMETOWN AFTER TOURING THESE TERRORS — A CITY WITH DARK, BONY DEPTHS, AN ISLAND OF HAUNTED DOLLS, ANCIENT STREETS HIDDEN UNDER MURKY WATERS AND TOWNS SWIRLING WITH AIR SO DEADLY YOU NEED A GAS MASK. YIKES!

POISONOUS RADIATION

In April 1986 there was an explosion at Chernobyl Nuclear Power Plant in modern-day Ukraine, eastern Europe. Deadly radiation (a special type of energy) leaked out and more than 49,000 people fled nearby Prypiat. It's still a ghost town — the radiation will remain for thousands of years.

UKRAINE

KINDA CREEPY · JEEPERS CREEPERS · CRAZY CREEPY

7

CREEP-O-METER

THE EMPIRE OF DEATH

WE'RE NOT TALKING ABOUT A COUPLE OF MOULDY OLD SKELETONS IN A SMALL TOMB. UNDER THE STREETS OF PARIS, THE BONES OF SIX MILLION PEOPLE LIE, STACKED IN TUNNELS THAT SPRAWL FOR KILOMETRES, AND BURROW AS DEEP AS A FIVE-STOREY BUILDING. DEEP UNDERGROUND, THE DUSTY ENTRANCE SIGN CALLS IT 'THE EMPIRE OF DEATH'.

THE PARIS CATACOMBS

When the graveyards of Paris, France, became full in the late 18th century, the dead were dug up and the bones transported by wagon at night. Their destination? The tunnels used for stone mining that criss-cross beneath the city. Over the years, more and more bones arrived at the catacombs. First, they were dumped in piles. Later, skulls and leg bones were arranged decoratively, until the tunnels were lined with a grim and grisly wallpaper, and bony columns and altars rose.

A LOCAL HISTORIAN REPORTS:

For a place of the dead, the tunnels have been lively over the years. In the 19th century, farmers grew mushrooms in them. During World War II, French Resistance fighters hid there, while German soldiers set up bunkers. Today, some adventurers, unconcerned about all the ghost stories, sneak into the tunnels through secret entrances all over the city. They prise off manhole covers and climb down through the sewers. In 2017 two teenage boys got lost down there. After three long days in the inky, dank darkness, rescue dogs found them. Phew!

KINDA CREEPY   JEEPERS CREEPERS   CRAZY CREEPY

7

CREEP-O-METER

DOLLS OF DREAD

LIKE A TOY SHOP FROM YOUR WORST NIGHTMARE, THIS MEXICAN ISLAND DRIPS WITH DECAYING DOLLS, SOME LIMBLESS, SOME BODY-LESS, ALL SUPPOSEDLY POSSESSED BY GHOSTLY SPIRITS. NAGORO IS ANOTHER TERRIBLE DREAM. MORE LIFE-SIZE DOLLS LIVE IN THIS FREAKY JAPANESE TOWN THAN HUMANS. WAKE ME UP, PLEASE!

THE ISLAND OF THE DOLLS

In the 1950s, so the story goes, a young girl drowned near a small island, south of Mexico City, Central America. When the island's caretaker, Julian Santana Barrera, found a doll in the water, he tied it to a tree as a sign of respect for the child. That's when the trouble started. Julian began to hear footsteps, whisperings and wailings at night. To calm the girl's spirit, he hung up more and more dolls and today, there are hundreds of them. Some locals swear the dolls' blank, staring eyes move from side to side, watching them.

SCARECROW VILLAGE

When the population of her once-thriving village fell to less than 40, Tsukimi Ayano devised an unusual plan. She began to make life-size dolls, some resembling real people who had died or moved away. The first was a scarecrow of her deceased father. Today, there are about 350 dolls in Nagoro, working in the fields, waiting at a bus stop, fishing or sitting silently in rows in the old abandoned school.

JEEPERS CREEPERS

KINDA CREEPY

CRAZY CREEPY

8

CREEP-O-METER

SWALLOWED BY SAND

Don't bother with a bucket and spade — Kolmanskop is no holiday destination. This town in Namibia, southwest Africa, does have sand, but it's more swallow-a-house-whole sand than sandcastle sand. And it's not called a ghost-town for nothing...

THE DESERT THAT DEVOURS

In 1908, Zacharia Lewala was clearing sand from a railway track when he found some strange stones. They were diamonds and they brought German miners rushing to this remote, desolate place. Soon there were shops, an ice factory, a bowling alley and mansions ringed by lush green lawns, kept alive by rail deliveries of water. But when more diamonds were discovered elsewhere, people began to leave. In the 1950s Kolmanskop was totally abandoned. The sand, no longer swept away each day, blew over the lawns, inched higher and higher up walls and crept through windows to fill houses.

NAMIBIA

A GHOST-HUNTER'S DIARY:

We tourists were told not to look for diamonds. No problem — I hunt for ghosts, not shiny rocks. About 800 miners worked hard here, so perhaps a few exhausted souls haunt the place? There are reports of eerie sensations in the butcher's shop, bodiless voices and ghostly figures. I saw and heard nothing — but my nose did start to bleed! Apparently that's common in a dry desert, but I'm not so sure. Anyway, this weird wilderness of sand is very creepy and even I was happy to leave as night fell.

KINDA CREEPY JEEPERS CREEPERS CRAZY CREEPY

6

CREEP-O-METER

TOXIC TERROR

IMAGINE SETTING OFF FROM MIYAKE VILLAGE TO HIKE THE TRAILS OF THIS BEAUTIFUL JAPANESE ISLAND, NESTLED IN THE WARM PHILIPPINE SEA. HAVE YOU PACKED BINOCULARS FOR BIRD-WATCHING? GREAT. RICE CRACKERS FOR A SNACK? GOOD. A GAS MASK FOR TOXIC GAS? NO? BUT THE SIRENS HAVE JUST STARTED TO WAIL! UH-OH...

DISASTER ZONE

Miyake Island, 180 kilometres south of Japan's capital Tokyo, is dominated by a huge and very active volcano, Mount Oyama. Over the years, lava flows have buried the homes around it, and taken many lives. Ever since an eruption in 2000, the volcano has constantly belched toxic gas. Loudspeakers all over the island shriek an alarm call when sulphur dioxide levels get too high, and residents must put on a gas mask and shelter indoors. If not, they will be stricken by coughing, burning skin and sore eyes.

KINDA CREEPY · JEEPERS CREEPERS · CRAZY CREEPY

6

CREEP-O-METER

JAPAN

A LOCAL REPORTS:

This is my home, but it's hard to love sometimes. In 1983, when I was a kid, Oyama erupted and my school, my home, my whole neighbourhood was wiped out by the dreadful fiery flow. So when the earthquakes began in the summer of 2000, we knew trouble was brewing. Oyama finally blew its top on 14 July, and all 3,600 of us had to evacuate. It pumped out so much toxic gas we couldn't return for five years. It's still gassy, but my mask will protect me, I hope...

WEIRD WATER

Forget about paddling merrily in gentle streams, we're going to plunge into toxic pools of acid, exploding lakes, rivers that disappear and wild oceans that suck ships and planes into oblivion. It's going to be wet, wild and very weird.

LAKE NATRON, TANZANIA

This lake, in East Africa, doesn't let go of its dead. Its salty water, rich in soda ash from nearby volcanoes, preserves the corpses of eagles, flamingos and bats. These stone-like statues keep watch over waters stained blood-red by bacteria. Petrifying!

TANZANIA

CREEP-O-METER

KINDA CREEPY · JEEPERS CREEPERS · CRAZY CREEPY

5

FREAKY FALLS

A GLACIER THAT BLEEDS? A RIVER THAT DISAPPEARS? THESE WEIRD WATERFALLS ARE FREAKY, SHRIEKY AND DOWNRIGHT SNEAKY.

THE DEVIL'S KETTLE

As the Brule River in Minnesota, USA, forks, one side tumbles down a small waterfall and the other side... well, no one quite knows what happens to the other side. The water simply pours into a deep, dark pothole (a 'kettle') and disappears. Underground channels are unlikely as the volcanic rock is too hard to be hollowed out by water, like limestone. Geologists poured pink dyes and ping pong balls into the Devil's Kettle, hoping they'd appear in a river or lake nearby. But the markers were never seen again...

USA

BLOOD FALLS

The mystery of the Taylor Glacier in Antarctica oozing blood-red water puzzled scientists for years after its discovery in 1911. At first, they wondered if a red, seaweed-like algae was to blame. We now know that the water is rich in iron. As it seeps out from an underground lake, the iron reacts with oxygen in the air. Rust forms and paints the waterfall red. So Blood Falls gets its colour from iron — just like real blood.

BERMUDA TRIANGLE

In a triangle of wild Atlantic ocean between the tip of Florida, USA, and the islands of Bermuda and Puerto Rico, dozens of ships and aircraft have vanished without a trace. Scientists say hurricanes, strong currents and human errors are to blame. Boring! Alien abduction would be far more exciting. Imagine if Columbus really had seen a UFO on his way to the Americas! Science does offer one wacky theory — the missing craft were destroyed by, um, burps...

FLORIDA

CAROLL A. DEERING

AVENGER AEROPLANE AND CREW

A GHOST SHIP AND THE LOST AVENGERS

In 1921, the cargo ship *Caroll A. Deering* was found battered on a beach. It had sailed through the Bermuda Triangle and its crew was nowhere to be seen. Twenty-four years later, five Avenger aeroplanes flew into the triangle and vanished forever. Scientists in Norway may have solved the mystery of such disappearances. They discovered giant ocean craters that release explosions of methane gas. Could these 'burps of death' bubble up and sink ships, then burst into the air to suffocate sailors and knock planes from the sky?

DIARY EXTRACT OF ITALIAN EXPLORER CHRISTOPHER COLUMBUS AS HE APPROACHED THE BAHAMAS ON HIS VOYAGE TO THE AMERICAS, 11 OCTOBER, 1492:

At the tenth hour of the night, I saw a light, although it was something so faint that I did not wish to affirm that it was land... It was seen once or twice [by others]. It was like a little wax candle that was being lifted up and was rising.

KINDA CREEPY   JEEPERS CREEPERS   CRAZY CREEPY

5

CREEP-O-METER

PUERTO RICO

USA, BERMUDA, PUERTO RICO

DEADLY LAKES

FANCY A DIP? WELL, DIP ELSEWHERE. THESE ACID POOLS WOULD MELT YOUR GOGGLES IN MINUTES. AND IF THE GASSY LAKE FEELS LIKE EXPLODING, FORGET GOGGLES — YOU'LL NEED A GAS MASK.

POOLS OF ACID

Cross the Danakil Depression, a plain in northern Ethiopia, East Africa, off your holiday list. The air smells of rotten eggs and is thick with toxic sulphur and chlorine. It's one of the driest, hottest places on Earth, often reaching 50 °C. But you can't cool off in the pools — they're boiling hot and highly acidic. Lying near the coast, the pools contain sea salt, which reacts with minerals in the magma just beneath the surface. The result? Crazy colours — salty sculptures of bright yellow and pools of turquoise and green.

THE LAKE THAT ERUPTS

A pocket of magma beneath Lake Nyos continually leaks carbon dioxide (CO_2) into the water and, in 1986, this build-up of gas had devastating consequences. Without warning, a huge cloud of CO_2 erupted from the lake, which is in Cameroon, Central Africa. More than one million tons of gas rose at about 100 kmph and swept into a nearby valley, suffocating 1,746 people. The eruption also sent a giant wave hurtling across the lake and turned its iron-rich waters a deep red.

KINDA CREEPY JEEPERS CREEPERS CRAZY CREEPY

4

CREEP-O-METER

THE GREAT BLUE HOLE

PUNCTURING THE SUNLIT WATERS OF THE CARIBBEAN SEA, OFF THE COAST OF BELIZE, CENTRAL AMERICA, IS A HUGE DARK CIRCLE, THE MONSTROUS MOUTH TO A STRANGE UNDERWATER WORLD. THE GREAT BLUE HOLE IS A VERTICAL CAVE, 125 METRES DEEP, AND ITS WATERS SWIRL WITH SHARKS, TOXIC GASES AND MYTHS OF MONSTERS...

FOSSIL GRAVEYARD

The floor of the sinkhole is littered with the skeletons of sea creatures that fell into its depths, and died from a lack of oxygen. There may be land creatures here, too, as the Great Blue Hole was once on land. Its formation began about 150,000 years ago, when sea levels were lower. The limestone was hollowed out by water that slowly dissolved the rock. Sinkholes nearby hold the fossils of prehistoric snakes, tortoises and humans. The Great Blue Hole could well be another such watery tomb.

BELIZE

A DIVER'S LOGBOOK:

Descending into the gloom, I tried not to think of local stories about Lusca, a giant, octopus-like sea monster. Suddenly, twisting dark shapes appeared! Lusca's tentacles? No, reef sharks! At 30 metres, the hole widened into a huge underwater cathedral, giant stalactites clinging to its rocky roof. I continued to 40 metres, still far above the layer of toxic hydrogen sulphide, and not even halfway to the bottom. Even at this depth, divers go mad, unable to tell up from down. It was time to get out while I still could.

LIGHT SHOWS

AS NIGHT FALLS, DARKNESS PAINTS OUR LAKES AND SEAS AN INKY BLACK. EXCEPT WHEN NATURE IGNORES THE RULES, TOSSING STARS INTO THE OCEAN AND CRACKING THE SKY WITH FEARSOME STREAKS OF LIGHT.

LIGHTNING LAKE

Welcome to the most electric place on Earth: Lake Maracaibo in Venezuela, South America. The lake is surrounded by mountain ridges that form a bowl, collecting a soup of warm air from the Caribbean Sea, cold air tumbling down from the Andes Mountains and moisture evaporating from the lake itself. There's a secret ingredient, too: methane gas bubbling up from underground oil fields. The mixture is electric, and for most of the year lightning forks across these skies for a record-breaking 10 hours every night! Yikes!

VENEZUELA

SEA OF STARS

If you took a night-time dip here in the sea around Vaadhoo Island in the Maldives, you'd leave a trail of sparkling lights like the glittering tail of a comet. For your sweeping arms and kicking legs would agitate thousands of plankton (tiny sea organisms), causing chemical reactions that produce a glow. The movement of waves lapping against the shore has the same effect, dotting the beach with sparkles. This is bioluminescence. Weird or wonderful?
You decide.

KINDA CREEPY · JEEPERS CREEPERS · CRAZY CREEPY

2

CREEP-O-METER

MALDIVES

BEASTLY ABODES

PUT AWAY YOUR SPOTTER'S GUIDE, WE'RE GOING TO PLACES WHERE YOU REALLY DON'T WANT TO SPOT ANYTHING. DESOLATE MOORS PROWLED BY THROAT-RIPPING BEASTS, DARK SEWERS INVADED BY SHADOWY CREATURES AND AN ISLAND INFESTED WITH THOUSANDS OF VENOMOUS VIPERS. BRING REPELLENT.

KINDA CREEPY JEEPERS CREEPERS CRAZY CREEPY

6

CREEP-O-METER

GOMANTONG CAVE, MALAYSIAN BORNEO

Millions of wrinkle-lipped bats hang from the damp ceiling of this Southeast-Asian cave. Below them, a carpet of writhing cockroaches feast on the bats' guano (droppings). The cave walls crawl with long-legged centipedes, freaky scorpions and huge spiders. Enter this cave, enter your worst nightmare.

MALAYSIAN BORNEO

SNAKE ISLAND

YOU MIGHT WANT TO AVOID THIS DREADFUL PLACE. THE CLUE'S IN THE NAME. QUEIMADA GRANDE, A ROCKY OUTCROP ABOUT 30 KILOMETRES OFF THE COAST OF BRAZIL IN SOUTH AMERICA, IS INFESTED WITH 4,000 VIPERS. BUT THAT'S NOT ALL — THE SNAKES ARE SO VENOMOUS, THEIR BITE CAN MELT FLESH.

BRAZIL

VICIOUS VIPERS

The golden lancehead pit viper, its head pointed like the tip of a lance (spear), was stranded here thousands of years ago, when sea levels rose to create an island. With no tasty mammals around, the snake adapted, climbing trees to hunt birds. Its venom became supercharged — to kill the birds instantly, before they flew away. The viper had no predators and its population grew and grew. But, as it lives nowhere else in the world, it is critically endangered.

I visit Snake Island regularly to observe the vipers. They're pretty big, up to 1.2 metres long. Only scientists like me can travel here — the island was closed to the public in 1985 because of the deadly serpents. But a lighthouse keeper lived here long ago. In the 1920s, some say, snakes slithered through the lighthouse windows and killed him and his family.

KINDA CREEPY   JEEPERS CREEPERS   CRAZY CREEPY

7

CREEP-O-METER

SPIDERTOWNS

ARE CREEPY-CRAWLIES CREEPY? DO SPIDERS MAKE YOUR SPINE TINGLE? NO? THEN YOU'VE PROBABLY NOT BATTLED THROUGH A 300-METRE-LONG COBWEB OR CHEWED ON A TARANTULA AS BIG AS YOUR HAND…

GIANT COBWEB

Every so often, this unlucky Greek beach on Aitoliko Lagoon is smothered by a giant silvery cobweb, several hundred metres long. The culprit is not one huge spider (phew), but thousands of small 'stretch spiders'. They aim to catch mosquitoes in their dense silky webs, not humans. But if you want to avoid getting tangled up, don't try swimming to safety — these small, light arachnids can run on water!

GREECE

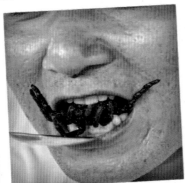

KINDA CREEPY · JEEPERS CREEPERS · CRAZY CREEPY

CREEP-O-METER

6

CAMBODIA

SPIDER SNACKS

Skuon is a town full of tasty snacks — if you like eating giant spiders, that is! Locals in the central Cambodian town catch them in nearby jungles, luring the tarantulas out of holes with sticks dipped in gasoline. The spiders are fried in oil with garlic and salt and piled high on trays, ready to be sold. At the meeting of two major roads, it's the perfect place for travellers to stop for a tasty tarantula. If you buy one, beware — sellers often keep a live tarantula on them for luck!

BEAST OF DARTMOOR

For hundreds of years, the dark, bleak moorlands of southwest England have inspired spooky folktales of ghosts, giants, witches and hounds from hell. But when the mutilated bodies of animals started turning up on the moors, a new creature of legend arose — the Beast of Dartmoor.

KINDA CREEPY JEEPERS CREEPERS CRAZY CREEPY

5

CREEP-O-METER

PANTHERS OR PUMAS?

Since the 1970s, many people have reported seeing big cats on the moor. Giant pawprints, deer shredded by razor-sharp claws, and sheep with their throats ripped out have been found. One story could explain these beastly discoveries. In 1978, Dartmoor Wildlife Park was due to receive five pumas from nearby Plymouth Zoo, which was closing. But only two pumas arrived. Some say Mary Chipperfield, the zoo's owner, not wanting to see her beloved pumas in another zoo, released the cats on the moor...

ENGLAND

FROM 'THE HOUND OF THE BASKERVILLES' (1902)
BY ARTHUR CONAN DOYLE, WHO WAS INSPIRED
BY DARTMOOR LEGENDS OF PHANTOM HOUNDS:

I sprang to my feet — my mind paralyzed by the dreadful shape which had sprung out upon us from the shadows of the fog. A hound it was, an enormous coal-black hound, but not such a hound as mortal eyes have ever seen. Fire burst from its open mouth, its eyes glowed with a smouldering glare... Could anything more savage, more appalling, more hellish be conceived than that dark form and savage face...

CROC-INFESTED SEWERS

Do monstrous crocs and alligators live in the murky depths of our sewers? Experts say unwanted pets, sometimes flushed down toilets into drains, wouldn't survive for long. But two stories from New York City and Paris will make you think twice about what lies beneath our city streets...

CROC-INFESTED SEWERS

On a cold February afternoon in 1935, a group of teenage boys were clearing snow, shovelling it into an open manhole in East Harlem, New York, USA. When Salvatore Condulucci knelt and peered into the drain, he saw something so shocking he almost fell in. 'It's an alligator!' he shouted. Sure enough, a 2-metre 'gator was thrashing around in the icy water. The boys looped a clothes-line around the beast's neck and pulled it out.

The alligator may have been transported by ship from its native southern state of Florida, fallen into the Harlem River, and swum into a drain.

USA

FRANCE

KINDA CREEPY · JEEPERS CREEPERS · CRAZY CREEPY

4

CREEP-O-METER

A CROCODILE NAMED ELEANORE

When something dark and scaly was spotted near the River Seine in Paris, France, in 1984, firefighters investigated, wading into the mucky waters of nearby sewers. There, swimming out of the gloom towards them, was a Nile crocodile! Herding it with brooms, they caught the beast and tied its mouth shut. The young reptile had probably been in the sewers for about two months, eating rats. Today, 'Eleanore' lives in an aquarium. Where she came from, no one really knows.

FRIGHT SITES

FANCY CHECKING OUT SOME HAUNTED HOUSES? OR FREAKILY DESERTED THEME PARKS? HOW ABOUT THE RUINS OF A HORROR-FILLED HOSPITAL OR A SPOOKY OLD PRISON GROANING WITH DARK SECRETS? NO, ME NEITHER. RUN AWAY WHILE YOU STILL CAN!

IRELAND

LEAP CASTLE, IRELAND

This castle, built in the 1400s or earlier, is not somewhere to hang out at night. A ghostly lady in red glides through the halls, clutching a dagger. There's also a foul-smelling beastly spirit, 'The Elemental', with claw-like fingers and black holes where eyes should be.

KINDA CREEPY · JEEPERS CREEPERS · CRAZY CREEPY

6

CREEP-O-METER

THE CHURCH OF BONES

THE CEMETERY CHURCH OF ALL SAINTS, ITS GOTHIC SPIRES RISING UP FROM THE GRAVESTONES, HOLDS A STRANGE SECRET IN THE GLOOMY DEPTHS OF ITS UNDERGROUND CHAPEL. THERE, DANGLING FROM CEILINGS, FRAMING ARCHES AND STACKED INTO ALMOST EVERY NOOK AND CRANNY ARE THE BONES OF MORE THAN 40,000 PEOPLE.

SKULL AND CROSSBONES

When the Black Death swept through Europe in the 14th century, the disease killed millions and this church's graveyard, in the town of Kutná Hora, Czech Republic, overflowed with the dead. About 100 years later, a half-blind monk dug up bodies to make more space. After he had stacked all the bones in pyramids in a chamber beneath the church, his sight was fully restored, so the legend goes. Others continued his grim decorations. By about 1870, chains of skulls criss-crossed the chamber and its gloom was lit by the candles of a giant chandelier made entirely from bones.

A BONE-CHILLING VISIT!

Last year, I took a night-time tour of this 'ossuary' (a container or room that stores the bones of the dead). By flickering candlelight, our tour guide, dressed as a monk, led us visitors down into the chamber. He urged us to keep quiet — to respect the dead and to enjoy being lost in the silence. I'm just glad I didn't get lost in the chamber!

KINDA CREEPY

JEEPERS CREEPERS

CRAZY CREEPY

5

CREEP-O-METER

HAUNTED HOUSES

LET'S TIPTOE IN TERROR AROUND AMERICA'S 'MOST HAUNTED HOUSE' AND A GHOULISHLY GRAND ENGLISH HALL WITH ONE VERY SPOOKY RESIDENT. THESE HAIR-RAISING HOMES ARE PACKED FULL OF HORRIBLE HISTORIES, AND STRANGE STORIES. ONCE UPON A TIME...

WAILING WHALEY HOUSE

Thomas Whaley built a house in San Diego, USA, on a site where the thief 'Yankee Jim' was once hanged. In 1857, he and his family moved in, and began to hear heavy footsteps — Jim's restless soul? Over the years, six of the Whaleys died in the house, one a baby. Some say the tragic family never left. Visitors report a baby wailing, empty chairs rocking, doors opening by themselves and ghostly phantoms in 19th-century clothes, playing in the dining room, sitting in the parlour and standing at the top of the stairs.

USA

ENGLAND

THE LADY OF WOLLATON HALL

In the dead of night, several people have seen a mysterious orange light glowing from room 19 at Wollaton Hall. But the house was empty, locked up after the tourists had left — with the electricity switched off. Built in the 1580s near Nottingham, the hall was once home to Lady Jane Middleton. Some say she fell from her horse and, paralyzed, was confined to her room, where she stayed until her death. The room number? Nineteen. It is said that Lady Jane's ghostly white figure stands among the towers on the roof, just above her old bedroom.

KINDA CREEPY · JEEPERS CREEPERS · CRAZY CREEPY

7

CREEP-O-METER

HAIR-RAISING HOSPITAL

IF YOU EVER FIND YOURSELF IN THE GERMAN TOWN OF BEELITZ, DON'T GET SICK. FOR THIS ABANDONED HOSPITAL WILL NOT MAKE YOU FEEL ANY BETTER. ITS ONCE-GRAND CORRIDORS ARE CRUMBLING WITH DECAY AND RUSTING MONSTERS OF MEDICAL EQUIPMENT LURK IN OLD OPERATING THEATERS. THIS PLACE IS SO CREEPY, YOUR EYEBALLS WILL POP OUT AND RUN AWAY SCREAMING.

GERMANY

SICK SOLDIERS

In 1902, the hospital opened its doors to patients with the lung disease tuberculosis (TB). When World War I erupted in 1914, the Red Cross turned the site into a military hospital, increasing the number of patient beds from 600 to about 1,500. In the 1990s, the hospital was gradually abandoned, the metal skeletons of its beds left to rust as the forest slowly reclaimed the site. Some say the anguished souls of the patients who suffered and died at the hospital never left...

A NURSE REPORTS:

Since the war broke out two years ago in 1914, I've been treating battlefield injuries — gunshot wounds, blindness caused by mustard gas, all kinds of horrors. One of my patients is a 27-year-old soldier. In October, during the Battle of the Somme in France, a shell (bomb) exploded, wounding his left thigh. After almost two months here recovering, he'll be released soon. His name? Adolf Hitler.

SCREAM PARKS

THESE AMUSEMENT PARKS DEFINITELY WON'T AMUSE. UNLESS YOU LIKE FRIGHT SITES ABANDONED TO DECAYING STATUES, SKELETONS OF ROLLER COASTERS AND SCARY-GO-ROUNDS TO SPIN YOU INTO A NIGHTMARE. FORGET THEME PARKS, THESE ARE SCREAM PARKS!

SINISTER SIX FLAGS

When Hurricane Katrina crashed into New Orleans, USA in 2005, it destroyed much of the city and, in the wider area, nearly 2,000 people lost their lives. The Six Flags amusement park was torn apart by the wild winds, and swamped with salty floodwater 2 metres deep. A month later, when the water finally receded, the park was beyond repair. Today, the abandoned site is so creepy that filmmakers shoot scary scenes among the rusting rollercoasters, and giant clown heads. But they had better watch out — alligators lurk among the ruins...

USA

KINDA CREEPY
JEEPERS CREEPERS
CRAZY CREEPY

6

CREEP-O-METER

GULLIVER'S CREEPY KINGDOM

In Jonathan Swift's 1726 novel, Gulliver washes up on Lilliput Island, and its tiny residents tie him down. In 1997, 'Gulliver's Kingdom' opened in Japan, complete with a 45-metre-long statue of Gulliver, but the park was unpopular. Were visitors put off by the statue's mad staring eyes or freaked out that the site was once the secret base of a murderous cult? After the park closed in 2001, it was visited only by urban explorers and photographers wanting to send chills down their own spines. But Gulliver wasn't allowed to rest in peace — the park and its bizarre giant statue were demolished in 2007.

PETRIFYING PRISON

THE EASTERN STATE PENITENTIARY IN PHILADELPHIA, USA WAS MEANT TO LOOK TERRIFYING. THE ARCHITECT DESIGNED THE PRISON TO LOOK LIKE A SPOOKY MEDIEVAL CASTLE IN ORDER TO 'STRIKE FEAR INTO THE HEARTS OF THOSE WHO THOUGHT OF COMMITTING A CRIME'.

EASTERN STATE PENITENTIARY

When its gates swung open for the first time in 1829, the prison was the largest, most expensive public building in the USA. Within its 9-metre-high walls, seven long cellblocks radiated from a central hall. From there, one guard could see all 450 cell doors. The gangster Al 'Scarface' Capone spent eight months there in 1929, furnishing his cell with paintings, fine rugs and a radio. Today, there is no such luxury. Abandoned towers crumble and ceilings drip with rainwater. And, if you believe the stories, strange shadows crawl along walls and the endless corridors echo with the crazed laughter and anguished screams of ghostly prisoners.

A PRISON WARDEN REPORTS:

A penitentiary makes prisoners 'penitent' — regretful of their crimes. It's the 1830s and we do this with solitude and silence. Our prisoners don't see or talk to anyone. They stay in their cells, and I shove food through a hatch. When someone has to leave his cell, I put a hood over his head. And if an inmate talks, I chain an iron gag around his head. If that doesn't shut him up, it's off to The Hole. A few days in a tiny, dark underground cell usually has a man begging for forgiveness.

KINDA CREEPY JEEPERS CREEPERS CRAZY CREEPY

7

CREEP-O-METER

The publishers would like to thank the following sources for their kind permission to reproduce the pictures in this book.

Pages 1 & 2-3: Leon Rafael/Shutterstock; 4-5: Tomasz Jocz/Shutterstock; 6-7 (background): Ioannis Ioannou/Shutterstock; 6 (left): Alasdair Turner/Getty Images; 6 (right): Ingo Oeland/Alamy Stock Photo; 7 (top left): Leonardo Papini/SambaPhoto; 7 (bottom right): Ayhan Mehmet/Anadolu Agency/Getty Images; 8-9: Lockenes/Shutterstock; 10-11 (background): fhm/Getty Images; 10-11 (bottom): Claire McAdams/Shutterstock; 10 (top left): Venus Kaewyoo/Shutterstock; 11 (top right): Sanjit Das/Bloomberg via Getty Images; 12-13 (background): GROGL/Shutterstock; 14-15 (background): TOMMOT/Shutterstock; 16-17 (background): Ingo Oeland/Alamy Stock Photo; 16 (top left): Ken Griffiths/Shutterstock; 16 (bottom right): Corbis via Getty Images; 18-19 (background): Carsten Peter/Speleoresearch & Films/Getty Images; 19 (top): Wangkun Jia/Shutterstock; 20-21: Tomasz Jocz/Shutterstock; 22-23 (background): Wyatt Rivard/Shutterstock; 22 (top left): Netfalls Remy Musser/Shutterstock; 23 (top right): javarman/Shutterstock; 23 (right): STILLFX/Shutterstock; 24-25 (background): avf71/Shutterstock; 24 (left): Leon Rafael/Shutterstock; 25 (top right): SOURCENEXT/Alamy Stock Photo; 26-27 (background) & 27 (top right): Lukas Bischoff Photograph/Shutterstock; 28-29 (background): The Asahi Shimbun via Getty Images; 28 (top left): andrea crisante/Shutterstock; 29 (top right): Newscom/Alamy Stock Photo; 30-31 (background): Stephen Schramm/Alamy Stock Photo; 30-31 (bird): Coryn/Shutterstock; 32-33 (background): Ramesh Pavvluri Veera/Shutterstock; 33 (top right): Alasdair Turner/Getty Images; 34-35 (background): Anton Balazh/Shutterstock; 34 (right): Bettmann/Getty Images; 34 (bottom right): The LIFE Picture Collection/Getty Images; 35 (centre): Everett Historical/Shutterstock; 36-37 (background): MANAMANA/Shutterstock; 37 (right): Thierry Orban/Sygma via Getty Images; 38-39 (background): Globe Guide Media Inc/Shutterstock; 39 (top right): Subphoto/Shutterstock; 39 (centre): frantisekhojdysz/Shutterstock; 39 (bottom): Matt9122/Shutterstock; 40-41 (background): Miguel Gutierrez/EPA-EFE/Shutterstock; 41 (top right): Doug Perrine/Nature Picture Library/Getty Images; 42-43 (background): Patrick Meier/Moment/Getty Images; 42-43 (top): All-stock-photos/Shutterstock; 42 (left): Minden Pictures/Alamy Stock Photo; 42 (bottom): Chris Howes/Wild Places Photography/Alamy Stock Photo; 43 (top): Eugeniu Birca/Shutterstock; 44-45 (background): Leonardo Papini/SambaPhoto/Getty Images; 44 (top left): aulia ananta/Shutterstock; 44 (top right): halimqd/Shutterstock; 44 (bottom left): Minden Pictures/Alamy Stock Photo; 45 (centre): Edson Campolina/Shutterstock; 46-47 (background): Ayhan Mehmet/Anadolu Agency/Getty Images; 47 (top centre, right & bottom left): Tang Chhin Sothy/AFP/Getty Images; 48-49 (beast): Anton_Ivanov/Shutterstock; 48-49 (Dartmoor background): Matt Amery/Shutterstock; 48-49 (mist): Claire McAdams/Shutterstock; 49 (top left): Granger/Shutterstock; 50-51 (manhole): GWoeii/Shutterstock; 50-51 (alligator): GTD7/Shutterstock; 50-51 (feet): Andrea Nissotti/Shutterstock; 50-51 (cap): Allan Cash Picture Library/Alamy Stock Photo; 50-51 (body): Valery Sidelnikov/Shutterstock; 50 (bottom right): Bettmann/Getty Images; 51 (top right): St. Nick/Shutterstock; 51 (right): Adrian Steller/Alamy Stock Photo; 51 (crocodile): Paco Como/Shutterstock; 52-53: Dontsu/Shutterstock; 54-55 (background): M. Borchi/DeAgostini/Getty Images; 54 (top left): W. Buss/DeAgostini/Getty Images; 55 (centre): Angelo Andreas Zinna/Alamy Stock Photo; 56-57 (background): Joseph S Giacalone/Alamy Stock Photo; 57 (top right): Tracey Whitefoot/Alamy Stock Photo; 58-59 (background): Nicole Kwiatkowski/Shutterstock; 59 (top right): PhotoPhilipp/Shutterstock; 60-61 (background): KEG-KEG/Shutterstock; 61 (top right): The Asahi Shimbun via Getty Images; 62-63 (background): Nagel Photography/Shutterstock; 63 (top right): Felix Mizioznikov/Shutterstock; 63 (right): Charles Walker Collection/Alamy Stock Photo; 64: Tomasz Jocz/Shutterstock.